FOR WOMEN

52 Favorite Bible Verses, Devotionals,
Prayer Requests, and Colorable
Bible Quotations

Flora Morris Brown
and Walstein Walker

Copyright © 2023 by Flora Morris Brown, Ph.D.

All rights reserved. No part of this book may be used or reproduced in any form or by any means electronic or mechanical, including photocopying, recording, or by any information storage and retrieval system now known or hereafter invented, without the express written permission of the primary author.

Printed in the United States of America
by
Sonata Press

Flora Morris Brown, Ph.D.
Primary Author

Walstein Walker
Contributing Author

ISBN: 978-0-9965794-4-5

Flora Brown Associates
and Sonata Press
17602-17th Street
Suite102, #1015
Tustin, California 92780

DEDICATION

We dedicate this book to our extraordinary mothers, Mildred Morris and Gertrude Thomas. Their lives were a true example of the indomitable strength and perseverance of the human soul during adversities. They exemplified the traits of the mightiest women in Bible history. Like Ruth, they were steadfast in their faithfulness and devotion; like Rachel, they faced adversity with unwavering strength; and like Miriam, they fiercely protected the innocent.

In spite of the struggles and obstacles they faced, their lasting faith in God's promises inspires and motivates us today. We wish that their heritage and example will inspire you and future generations.

HOW TO USE THIS JOURNAL

Congratulations for making time to immerse yourself in the living Word of God. This is one of the best things you can do to grow your faith or even rediscover it.

This journal is designed to be reviewed at your own pace, but it can also be used in Bible study with your family or church group. We have used the King James Version, but we encourage you to refer to your favorite version of the Bible to review the 52 Bible verses we have provided. Focus on one or several passages to help you remember, reflect, and meditate on the messages, healings, and miracles God has provided throughout the ages.

The format used is based on Lectio Divina, a centuries-old, contemplative Bible reading method which consists of four parts: Lectio Divina commonly has 4 parts: Lectio (reading), Meditatio (meditation), Oratio (prayer), and Contemplatio (contemplation).

Do not be intimidated by the Latin words of this method. Create a quiet space to study. Then get still, permit the words to permeate your being, and respond as you are moved to do so.

In addition to the devotionals, enjoy the prayer requests, colorable scriptures, and other activities to reflect on and strengthen your spiritual life.

Embark on this spiritual journey with courage and an open heart, for it has the power to transform your life and fill it with boundless hope, faith, and joy.

ABOUT THE AUTHORS

Walstein Walker and Flora Brown are two longtime friends who collaborated to create this prayer journal for women. Their friendship began in the 1960s when they taught a Sunday School class together at a church in Los Angeles, California. Walstein's artistic talent and Flora's writing skills made them an unbeatable pair creating activities to engage and inspire their young students and each other.

Even though their families grew larger and kept them increasingly busy, they remained close friends through the years and continued to inspire each other with scriptures and prayers. They created this journal to share with you their favorite scriptures and ways to study them. They believe the scriptures and activities they have shared will uplift, inspire, and comfort you, just as they have done for the two of them.

ALSO BY FLORA MORRIS BROWN, PH.D.

Journal for a Phenomenal Woman

Redesigning my Resilient Life: A Guided Journal for the Pandemic, Social Unrest, Political Turmoil

Color Your Life Happy: Create Your Unique Path and Claim the Joy You Deserve

The Color Your Life Happy Gratitude Journal

The Color Your Life Happy Do It Your Way Journal

Slow Cooker Recipes for Potlucks and Parties

Mother's Day Recipes: 30 Kid-Friendly and Dad-Approved Ways to Impress and Delight Mom

Getting Unstuck: How to Get Your Confidence Back and Follow Your Dream

Memorable Poems and Unremarkable Verse

Color Your Life Happy Coloring Book for Adults

See the full listing of books and journals
by Flora Morris Brown, Ph.D.
at
amazon.com/author/florabrown

YOUR READING

✣

Proverbs 3:5—6

"Trust in the Lord with all thine heart; and lean not unto thine own understanding. In all thy ways acknowledge him, and he shall direct thy paths."

✣

Before you begin, take a moment to prepare your heart and mind.

Get in a quiet space. Clear your mind. Pray and invite God into this time.

Slowly read the Bible passage several times. Take your time.

Read quietly. Read out loud. Write it down.

_____
_____
_____

Note the words or phrases that speak to you.

Do not analyze. Just notice them.

Reflect on the word or phrases. What do they bring to mind?

Ask God to clarify and speak clearly to you.

_____
_____
_____

Put your pen down. Sit quietly and listen for any new thoughts or what you sense the Lord is asking of you.

Respond with a written prayer of praise and thanksgiving.

_____
_____
_____
_____

YOUR READING

✢

1 Corinthians 2:5

"That your faith should not stand in the wisdom of men,
but in the power of God."

✢

Before you begin, take a moment to prepare your heart and mind.
Get in a quiet space. Clear your mind. Pray and invite God into this time.

Slowly read the Bible passage several times. Take your time.
Read quietly. Read out loud. Write it down.

_____
_____
_____

Note the words or phrases that speak to you.
Do not analyze. Just notice them.

Reflect on the word or phrases. What do they bring to mind?
Ask God to clarify and speak clearly to you.

_____
_____
_____

Put your pen down. Sit quietly and listen for any new thoughts or what you sense the Lord is asking of you.

Respond with a written prayer of praise and thanksgiving.

_____
_____
_____
_____

Prayer Request

Date: _____

_____
_____
_____
_____

Answered Prayer

Date: _____

_____
_____
_____
_____

Reflections

Date: _____

_____
_____
_____
_____

YOUR READING

✣

John 14:27

"Peace I leave with you, my peace I give unto you: not as the world giveth, give I unto you. Let not your heart be troubled, neither let it be afraid."

✣

Before you begin, take a moment to prepare your heart and mind.

Get in a quiet space. Clear your mind. Pray and invite God into this time.

Slowly read the Bible passage several times. Take your time.

Read quietly. Read out loud. Write it down.

_____
_____
_____

Note the words or phrases that speak to you.

Do not analyze. Just notice them.

Reflect on the word or phrases. What do they bring to mind?

Ask God to clarify and speak clearly to you.

_____
_____
_____

Put your pen down. Sit quietly and listen for any new thoughts or what you sense the Lord is asking of you.

Respond with a written prayer of praise and thanksgiving.

_____
_____
_____
_____

Prayer Request

Date: _____

_____
_____
_____
_____

Answered Prayer

Date: _____

_____
_____
_____
_____

Reflections

Date: _____

_____
_____
_____
_____

YOUR READING

Colossians 1:27

"To whom God would make known what is the riches of the glory of this mystery among the Gentiles; which is Christ in you, the hope of glory."

Before you begin, take a moment to prepare your heart and mind.
Get in a quiet space. Clear your mind. Pray and invite God into this time.

Slowly read the Bible passage several times. Take your time.
Read quietly. Read out loud. Write it down.

_____
_____
_____

Note the words or phrases that speak to you.
Do not analyze. Just notice them.

Reflect on the word or phrases. What do they bring to mind?
Ask God to clarify and speak clearly to you.

_____
_____
_____

Put your pen down. Sit quietly and listen for any new thoughts or what you sense the Lord is asking of you.

Respond with a written prayer of praise and thanksgiving.

_____
_____
_____
_____

Prayer Request

Date: _____

_____
_____
_____
_____

Answered Prayer

Date: _____

_____
_____
_____
_____

Reflections

Date: _____

_____
_____
_____
_____

YOUR READING

�֎

1 Corinthians 13:13
"And now abideth faith, hope, charity, these three;
but the greatest of these is charity."

�֎

Before you begin, take a moment to prepare your heart and mind.
Get in a quiet space. Clear your mind. Pray and invite God into this time.

Slowly read the Bible passage several times. Take your time.
Read quietly. Read out loud. Write it down.

_____
_____
_____

Note the words or phrases that speak to you.
Do not analyze. Just notice them.

Reflect on the word or phrases. What do they bring to mind?
Ask God to clarify and speak clearly to you.

_____
_____
_____

Put your pen down. Sit quietly and listen for any new thoughts or what you sense the Lord is asking of you.

Respond with a written prayer of praise and thanksgiving.

_____
_____
_____
_____

YOUR READING

✤

1 Corinthians 16:13

"Watch ye, stand fast in the faith, quit you like men, be strong."

✤

Before you begin, take a moment to prepare your heart and mind.
Get in a quiet space. Clear your mind. Pray and invite God into this time.

Slowly read the Bible passage several times. Take your time.
Read quietly. Read out loud. Write it down.

_____
_____
_____

Note the words or phrases that speak to you.
Do not analyze. Just notice them.

Reflect on the word or phrases. What do they bring to mind?
Ask God to clarify and speak clearly to you.

_____
_____
_____

Put your pen down. Sit quietly and listen for any new thoughts or what you sense the Lord is asking of you.

Respond with a written prayer of praise and thanksgiving.

_____
_____
_____
_____

Prayer Request

Date: _____

_____
_____
_____
_____

Answered Prayer

Date: _____

_____
_____
_____
_____

Reflections

Date: _____

_____
_____
_____
_____

YOUR READING

✣

Romans 15:13

"Now the God of hope fill you with all joy and peace in believing, that ye may abound in hope, through the power of the Holy Ghost."

✣

Before you begin, take a moment to prepare your heart and mind.
Get in a quiet space. Clear your mind. Pray and invite God into this time.

Slowly read the Bible passage several times. Take your time.
Read quietly. Read out loud. Write it down.

_____
_____
_____

Note the words or phrases that speak to you.
Do not analyze. Just notice them.

Reflect on the word or phrases. What do they bring to mind?
Ask God to clarify and speak clearly to you.

_____
_____
_____

Put your pen down. Sit quietly and listen for any new thoughts or what you sense the Lord is asking of you.

Respond with a written prayer of praise and thanksgiving.

_____
_____
_____
_____

YOUR READING

✥

Hebrews 11:6

"But without faith it is impossible to please him: for he that cometh to God must believe that he is a rewarder of them that diligently seek him."

✥

Before you begin, take a moment to prepare your heart and mind.

Get in a quiet space. Clear your mind. Pray and invite God into this time.

Slowly read the Bible passage several times. Take your time.

Read quietly. Read out loud. Write it down.

_____
_____
_____

Note the words or phrases that speak to you.

Do not analyze. Just notice them.

Reflect on the word or phrases. What do they bring to mind?

Ask God to clarify and speak clearly to you.

_____
_____
_____

Put your pen down. Sit quietly and listen for any new thoughts or what you sense the Lord is asking of you.

Respond with a written prayer of praise and thanksgiving.

_____
_____
_____
_____

Times I stepped out on faith

List the times you were afraid, but trusted God and you succeeded

_____
_____
_____
_____
_____
_____
_____
_____
_____
_____
_____
_____
_____
_____
_____
_____
_____
_____

YOUR READING

✤

Psalm 30:5

"For his anger endureth but a moment; in his favour is life: weeping may endure for a night, but joy cometh in the morning."

✤

Before you begin, take a moment to prepare your heart and mind.

Get in a quiet space. Clear your mind. Pray and invite God into this time.

Slowly read the Bible passage several times. Take your time.

Read quietly. Read out loud. Write it down.

_____
_____
_____

Note the words or phrases that speak to you.

Do not analyze. Just notice them.

Reflect on the word or phrases. What do they bring to mind?

Ask God to clarify and speak clearly to you.

_____
_____
_____

Put your pen down. Sit quietly and listen for any new thoughts or what you sense the Lord is asking of you.

Respond with a written prayer of praise and thanksgiving.

_____
_____
_____
_____

Ways God has blessed me

_____
_____
_____
_____
_____
_____
_____
_____
_____
_____
_____
_____
_____
_____
_____

YOUR READING

—— ——

Matthew 21:22

"And all things whatsoever ye shall ask in prayer, believing, ye shall receive."

—— ✣ ——

Before you begin, take a moment to prepare your heart and mind.
Get in a quiet space. Clear your mind. Pray and invite God into this time.

Slowly read the Bible passage several times. Take your time.
Read quietly. Read out loud. Write it down.

_____
_____
_____

Note the words or phrases that speak to you.
Do not analyze. Just notice them.

Reflect on the word or phrases. What do they bring to mind?
Ask God to clarify and speak clearly to you.

_____
_____
_____

Put your pen down. Sit quietly and listen for any new thoughts or what you sense the Lord is asking of you.

Respond with a written prayer of praise and thanksgiving.

_____
_____
_____
_____

YOUR READING

─── ───

Psalm 41:1

"Blessed is he that considereth the poor;
the Lord will deliver him in time of trouble."

─── ✜ ───

Before you begin, take a moment to prepare your heart and mind.

Get in a quiet space. Clear your mind. Pray and invite God into this time.

Slowly read the Bible passage several times. Take your time.

Read quietly. Read out loud. Write it down.

_____

_____

_____

Note the words or phrases that speak to you.

Do not analyze. Just notice them.

Reflect on the word or phrases. What do they bring to mind?

Ask God to clarify and speak clearly to you.

_____

_____

_____

Put your pen down. Sit quietly and listen for any new thoughts or what you sense the Lord is asking of you.

Respond with a written prayer of praise and thanksgiving.

_____

_____

_____

_____

Prayer Request

Date: _____

_____
_____
_____
_____

Answered Prayer

Date: _____

_____
_____
_____
_____

Reflections

Date: _____

_____
_____
_____
_____

YOUR READING

—— ✠ ——

Psalm 118:24

"This is the day which the Lord hath made;
We will rejoice and be glad in it."

—— ✠ ——

Before you begin, take a moment to prepare your heart and mind.

Get in a quiet space. Clear your mind. Pray and invite God into this time.

Slowly read the Bible passage several times. Take your time.

Read quietly. Read out loud. Write it down.

_____
_____
_____

Note the words or phrases that speak to you.

Do not analyze. Just notice them.

Reflect on the word or phrases. What do they bring to mind?

Ask God to clarify and speak clearly to you.

_____
_____
_____

Put your pen down. Sit quietly and listen for any new thoughts or what you sense the Lord is asking of you.

Respond with a written prayer of praise and thanksgiving.

_____
_____
_____
_____

Lord, help me to

People I'm praying for today

YOUR READING

✠

Psalm 46:1

"God is our refuge and strength, a very present help in trouble."

✠

Before you begin, take a moment to prepare your heart and mind.
Get in a quiet space. Clear your mind. Pray and invite God into this time.

Slowly read the Bible passage several times. Take your time.
Read quietly. Read out loud. Write it down.

_____
_____
_____

Note the words or phrases that speak to you.
Do not analyze. Just notice them.

Reflect on the word or phrases. What do they bring to mind?
Ask God to clarify and speak clearly to you.

_____
_____
_____

Put your pen down. Sit quietly and listen for any new thoughts or what you sense the Lord is asking of you.

Respond with a written prayer of praise and thanksgiving.

_____
_____
_____
_____

Times I stepped out on faith

List the times you were afraid, but trusted God and you succeeded

_____
_____
_____
_____
_____
_____
_____
_____
_____
_____
_____
_____
_____
_____
_____
_____
_____

YOUR READING

Psalm 31:24

"Be of good courage, and he shall strengthen your heart,
all ye that hope in the LORD."

Before you begin, take a moment to prepare your heart and mind.
Get in a quiet space. Clear your mind. Pray and invite God into this time.

Slowly read the Bible passage several times. Take your time.
Read quietly. Read out loud. Write it down.

_____
_____
_____

Note the words or phrases that speak to you.
Do not analyze. Just notice them.

Reflect on the word or phrases. What do they bring to mind?
Ask God to clarify and speak clearly to you.

_____
_____
_____

Put your pen down. Sit quietly and listen for any new thoughts or what you sense the Lord is asking of you.

Respond with a written prayer of praise and thanksgiving.

_____
_____
_____
_____

Ways God has blessed me

_____
_____
_____
_____
_____
_____
_____
_____
_____
_____
_____
_____
_____
_____
_____
_____
_____
_____

YOUR READING

✢

1 Thessalonians 5:17

"Pray without ceasing."

✢

Before you begin, take a moment to prepare your heart and mind.

Get in a quiet space. Clear your mind. Pray and invite God into this time.

Slowly read the Bible passage several times. Take your time.

Read quietly. Read out loud. Write it down.

_____
_____
_____

Note the words or phrases that speak to you.

Do not analyze. Just notice them.

Reflect on the word or phrases. What do they bring to mind?

Ask God to clarify and speak clearly to you.

_____
_____
_____

Put your pen down. Sit quietly and listen for any new thoughts or what you sense the Lord is asking of you.

Respond with a written prayer of praise and thanksgiving.

_____
_____
_____
_____

YOUR READING

✤

Matthew 25:21

"His lord said unto him, Well done, thou good and faithful servant: thou hast been faithful over a few things, I will make thee ruler over many things: enter thou into the joy of thy lord."

✤

Before you begin, take a moment to prepare your heart and mind.

Get in a quiet space. Clear your mind. Pray and invite God into this time.

Slowly read the Bible passage several times. Take your time.

Read quietly. Read out loud. Write it down.

_____
_____
_____

Note the words or phrases that speak to you.

Do not analyze. Just notice them.

Reflect on the word or phrases. What do they bring to mind?

Ask God to clarify and speak clearly to you.

_____
_____
_____

Put your pen down. Sit quietly and listen for any new thoughts or what you sense the Lord is asking of you.

Respond with a written prayer of praise and thanksgiving.

_____
_____
_____
_____

Prayer Request

Date: _____

_____
_____
_____
_____

Answered Prayer

Date: _____

_____
_____
_____
_____

Reflections

Date: _____

_____
_____
_____
_____

YOUR READING

✣

James 1:5

"If any of you lack wisdom, let him ask of God, that giveth to all men liberally and upbraideth not; and it shall be given him."

✣

Before you begin, take a moment to prepare your heart and mind.

Get in a quiet space. Clear your mind. Pray and invite God into this time.

Slowly read the Bible passage several times. Take your time.

Read quietly. Read out loud. Write it down.

_____
_____
_____

Note the words or phrases that speak to you.

Do not analyze. Just notice them.

Reflect on the word or phrases. What do they bring to mind?

Ask God to clarify and speak clearly to you.

_____
_____
_____

Put your pen down. Sit quietly and listen for any new thoughts or what you sense the Lord is asking of you.

Respond with a written prayer of praise and thanksgiving.

_____
_____
_____
_____

YOUR READING

✢

Romans 12:15

"Rejoice with them that do rejoice, and weep with them that weep."

✢

Before you begin, take a moment to prepare your heart and mind.

Get in a quiet space. Clear your mind. Pray and invite God into this time.

Slowly read the Bible passage several times. Take your time.

Read quietly. Read out loud. Write it down.

_____
_____
_____

Note the words or phrases that speak to you.

Do not analyze. Just notice them.

Reflect on the word or phrases. What do they bring to mind?

Ask God to clarify and speak clearly to you.

_____
_____
_____

Put your pen down. Sit quietly and listen for any new thoughts or what you sense the Lord is asking of you.

Respond with a written prayer of praise and thanksgiving.

_____
_____
_____
_____

Lord, help me to

People I'm praying for today

YOUR READING

✠

Psalm 81:1

"Sing aloud unto God our strength:
make a joyful noise unto the God of Jacob."

✠

Before you begin, take a moment to prepare your heart and mind.

Get in a quiet space. Clear your mind. Pray and invite God into this time.

Slowly read the Bible passage several times. Take your time.

Read quietly. Read out loud. Write it down.

_____
_____
_____

Note the words or phrases that speak to you.

Do not analyze. Just notice them.

Reflect on the word or phrases. What do they bring to mind?

Ask God to clarify and speak clearly to you.

_____
_____
_____

Put your pen down. Sit quietly and listen for any new thoughts or what you sense the Lord is asking of you.

Respond with a written prayer of praise and thanksgiving.

_____
_____
_____
_____

Times I stepped out on faith

List the times you were afraid, but trusted God and you succeeded

YOUR READING

✜

Proverbs 15:1—2

"A soft answer turneth away wrath: but grievous words stir up anger. The tongue of the wise useth knowledge aright: but the mouth of fools poureth out foolishness."

✜

Before you begin, take a moment to prepare your heart and mind.

Get in a quiet space. Clear your mind. Pray and invite God into this time.

Slowly read the Bible passage several times. Take your time.

Read quietly. Read out loud. Write it down.

_____
_____
_____

Note the words or phrases that speak to you.

Do not analyze. Just notice them.

Reflect on the word or phrases. What do they bring to mind?

Ask God to clarify and speak clearly to you.

_____
_____
_____

Put your pen down. Sit quietly and listen for any new thoughts or what you sense the Lord is asking of you.

Respond with a written prayer of praise and thanksgiving.

_____
_____
_____
_____

Ways God has blessed me

_____
_____
_____
_____
_____
_____
_____
_____
_____
_____
_____
_____
_____
_____
_____
_____
_____

YOUR READING

Galatians 5:22

"But the fruit of the Spirit is love, joy, peace, long-suffering, gentleness, goodness, faith."

Before you begin, take a moment to prepare your heart and mind.
Get in a quiet space. Clear your mind. Pray and invite God into this time.

Slowly read the Bible passage several times. Take your time.
Read quietly. Read out loud. Write it down.

_____
_____
_____

Note the words or phrases that speak to you.
Do not analyze. Just notice them.

Reflect on the word or phrases. What do they bring to mind?
Ask God to clarify and speak clearly to you.

_____
_____
_____

Put your pen down. Sit quietly and listen for any new thoughts or what you sense the Lord is asking of you.

Respond with a written prayer of praise and thanksgiving.

_____
_____
_____
_____

Lord, help me to

People I'm praying for today

YOUR READING

✠

Ephesians 2:8—9
"For by grace are ye saved through faith: and that not of yourselves:
it is the gift of God: Not of works, lest any man should boast."

✠

Before you begin, take a moment to prepare your heart and mind.
Get in a quiet space. Clear your mind. Pray and invite God into this time.

Slowly read the Bible passage several times. Take your time.
Read quietly. Read out loud. Write it down.

_____
_____
_____

Note the words or phrases that speak to you.
Do not analyze. Just notice them.

Reflect on the word or phrases. What do they bring to mind?
Ask God to clarify and speak clearly to you.

_____
_____
_____

Put your pen down. Sit quietly and listen for any new thoughts or what you sense the Lord is asking of you.

Respond with a written prayer of praise and thanksgiving.

_____
_____
_____
_____

Times I stepped out on faith

List the times you were afraid, but trusted God and you succeeded

_____
_____
_____
_____
_____
_____
_____
_____
_____
_____
_____
_____
_____
_____
_____
_____
_____

YOUR READING

✠

Romans 8:28

"And we know that all things work together for good to them that love God, to them who are the called according to his purpose."

✠

Before you begin, take a moment to prepare your heart and mind.

Get in a quiet space. Clear your mind. Pray and invite God into this time.

Slowly read the Bible passage several times. Take your time.

Read quietly. Read out loud. Write it down.

_____
_____
_____

Note the words or phrases that speak to you.

Do not analyze. Just notice them.

Reflect on the word or phrases. What do they bring to mind?

Ask God to clarify and speak clearly to you.

_____
_____
_____

Put your pen down. Sit quietly and listen for any new thoughts or what you sense the Lord is asking of you.

Respond with a written prayer of praise and thanksgiving.

_____
_____
_____
_____

Ways God has blessed me

_____
_____
_____
_____
_____
_____
_____
_____
_____
_____
_____
_____
_____
_____
_____
_____
_____
_____

YOUR READING

✢

Matthew 6:33

"But seek ye first the kingdom of God, and his righteousness; and all these things shall be added unto you."

✢

Before you begin, take a moment to prepare your heart and mind.

Get in a quiet space. Clear your mind. Pray and invite God into this time.

Slowly read the Bible passage several times. Take your time.

Read quietly. Read out loud. Write it down.

_____

_____

_____

Note the words or phrases that speak to you.

Do not analyze. Just notice them.

Reflect on the word or phrases. What do they bring to mind?

Ask God to clarify and speak clearly to you.

_____

_____

_____

Put your pen down. Sit quietly and listen for any new thoughts or what you sense the Lord is asking of you.

Respond with a written prayer of praise and thanksgiving.

_____

_____

_____

_____

Lord, help me to

People I'm praying for today

YOUR READING

Psalm 100:1—2

"Make a joyful noise unto the Lord, all ye lands. Serve the Lord with gladness. Come before his presence with singing."

Before you begin, take a moment to prepare your heart and mind.

Get in a quiet space. Clear your mind. Pray and invite God into this time.

Slowly read the Bible passage several times. Take your time.

Read quietly. Read out loud. Write it down.

_____
_____
_____

Note the words or phrases that speak to you.

Do not analyze. Just notice them.

Reflect on the word or phrases. What do they bring to mind?

Ask God to clarify and speak clearly to you.

_____
_____
_____

Put your pen down. Sit quietly and listen for any new thoughts or what you sense the Lord is asking of you.

Respond with a written prayer of praise and thanksgiving.

_____
_____
_____
_____

Times I stepped out on faith

List the times you were afraid, but trusted God and you succeeded

YOUR READING

------

Philippians 4:13

"I can do all things through Christ which strengtheneth me."

Before you begin, take a moment to prepare your heart and mind.
Get in a quiet space. Clear your mind. Pray and invite God into this time.

Slowly read the Bible passage several times. Take your time.
Read quietly. Read out loud. Write it down.

_____
_____
_____

Note the words or phrases that speak to you.
Do not analyze. Just notice them.

Reflect on the word or phrases. What do they bring to mind?
Ask God to clarify and speak clearly to you.

_____
_____
_____

Put your pen down. Sit quietly and listen for any new thoughts or what you sense the Lord is asking of you.

Respond with a written prayer of praise and thanksgiving.

_____
_____
_____
_____

YOUR READING

✜

Isaiah 26:3

"Thou wilt keep him in perfect peace, whose mind is stayed on thee: because he trusteth in thee."

✜

Before you begin, take a moment to prepare your heart and mind.

Get in a quiet space. Clear your mind. Pray and invite God into this time.

Slowly read the Bible passage several times. Take your time.

Read quietly. Read out loud. Write it down.

_____
_____
_____

Note the words or phrases that speak to you.

Do not analyze. Just notice them.

Reflect on the word or phrases. What do they bring to mind?

Ask God to clarify and speak clearly to you.

_____
_____
_____

Put your pen down. Sit quietly and listen for any new thoughts or what you sense the Lord is asking of you.

Respond with a written prayer of praise and thanksgiving.

_____
_____
_____
_____

YOUR READING

✜

Matthew 11:28—29

"Come unto me, all ye that labour and are heavy laden, and I will give you rest. Take my yoke upon you, and learn of me; for I am meek and lowly in heart: and ye shall find rest unto your souls."

✜

Before you begin, take a moment to prepare your heart and mind.

Get in a quiet space. Clear your mind. Pray and invite God into this time.

Slowly read the Bible passage several times. Take your time.

Read quietly. Read out loud. Write it down.

_____

_____

_____

Note the words or phrases that speak to you.

Do not analyze. Just notice them.

Reflect on the word or phrases. What do they bring to mind?

Ask God to clarify and speak clearly to you.

_____

_____

_____

Put your pen down. Sit quietly and listen for any new thoughts or what you sense the Lord is asking of you.

Respond with a written prayer of praise and thanksgiving.

_____

_____

_____

_____

Prayer Request

Date: _____

_____
_____
_____
_____

Answered Prayer

Date: _____

_____
_____
_____
_____

Reflections

Date: _____

_____
_____
_____
_____

YOUR READING

✥

Lamentations 3:22

"It is of the Lord's mercies that we are not consumed, because his compassions fail not. They are new every morning: great is thy faithfulness."

✥

Before you begin, take a moment to prepare your heart and mind.
Get in a quiet space. Clear your mind. Pray and invite God into this time.

Slowly read the Bible passage several times. Take your time.
Read quietly. Read out loud. Write it down.

_____
_____
_____

Note the words or phrases that speak to you.
Do not analyze. Just notice them.

Reflect on the word or phrases. What do they bring to mind?
Ask God to clarify and speak clearly to you.

_____
_____
_____

Put your pen down. Sit quietly and listen for any new thoughts or what you sense the Lord is asking of you.

Respond with a written prayer of praise and thanksgiving.

_____
_____
_____
_____

Lord, help me to

People I'm praying for today

YOUR READING

✤

Psalm 55:22

"Cast thy burden upon the Lord, and he shall sustain thee: he shall never suffer the righteous to be moved."

✤

Before you begin, take a moment to prepare your heart and mind.
Get in a quiet space. Clear your mind. Pray and invite God into this time.

Slowly read the Bible passage several times. Take your time.
Read quietly. Read out loud. Write it down.

_____
_____
_____

Note the words or phrases that speak to you.
Do not analyze. Just notice them.

Reflect on the word or phrases. What do they bring to mind?
Ask God to clarify and speak clearly to you.

_____
_____
_____

Put your pen down. Sit quietly and listen for any new thoughts or what you sense the Lord is asking of you.

Respond with a written prayer of praise and thanksgiving.

_____
_____
_____
_____

YOUR READING

---✣---

Isaiah 1:19

"If ye be willing and obedient, ye shall eat the good of the land."

---✣---

Before you begin, take a moment to prepare your heart and mind.

Get in a quiet space. Clear your mind. Pray and invite God into this time.

Slowly read the Bible passage several times. Take your time.

Read quietly. Read out loud. Write it down.

_____
_____
_____

Note the words or phrases that speak to you.

Do not analyze. Just notice them.

Reflect on the word or phrases. What do they bring to mind?

Ask God to clarify and speak clearly to you.

_____
_____
_____

Put your pen down. Sit quietly and listen for any new thoughts or what you sense the Lord is asking of you.

Respond with a written prayer of praise and thanksgiving.

_____
_____
_____
_____

YOUR READING

✤

Psalm 121:1—2

"I will lift up mine eyes unto the hills, from whence cometh my help.

My help cometh from the Lord, which made heaven and earth."

✤

Before you begin, take a moment to prepare your heart and mind.

Get in a quiet space. Clear your mind. Pray and invite God into this time.

Slowly read the Bible passage several times. Take your time.

Read quietly. Read out loud. Write it down.

_____
_____
_____

Note the words or phrases that speak to you.

Do not analyze. Just notice them.

Reflect on the word or phrases. What do they bring to mind?

Ask God to clarify and speak clearly to you.

_____
_____
_____

Put your pen down. Sit quietly and listen for any new thoughts or what you sense the Lord is asking of you.

Respond with a written prayer of praise and thanksgiving.

_____
_____
_____
_____

Prayer Request

Date: _____

_____
_____
_____

Answered Prayer

Date: _____

_____
_____
_____

Reflections

Date: _____

_____
_____
_____

YOUR READING

✤

Galatians 6:9

"And let us not be weary in well doing: for in due season we shall reap, if we faint not."

✤

Before you begin, take a moment to prepare your heart and mind.
Get in a quiet space. Clear your mind. Pray and invite God into this time.

Slowly read the Bible passage several times. Take your time.
Read quietly. Read out loud. Write it down.

_____
_____
_____

Note the words or phrases that speak to you.
Do not analyze. Just notice them.

Reflect on the word or phrases. What do they bring to mind?
Ask God to clarify and speak clearly to you.

_____
_____
_____

Put your pen down. Sit quietly and listen for any new thoughts or what you sense the Lord is asking of you.

Respond with a written prayer of praise and thanksgiving.

_____
_____
_____
_____

Lord, help me to

People I'm praying for today

YOUR READING

✜

Deuteronomy 31:6

"Be strong and of a good courage, fear not, nor be afraid of them: for the Lord thy God, he it is that doth go with thee; he will not fail thee, nor forsake thee."

✜

Before you begin, take a moment to prepare your heart and mind.

Get in a quiet space. Clear your mind. Pray and invite God into this time.

Slowly read the Bible passage several times. Take your time.

Read quietly. Read out loud. Write it down.

_____

_____

_____

Note the words or phrases that speak to you.

Do not analyze. Just notice them.

Reflect on the word or phrases. What do they bring to mind?

Ask God to clarify and speak clearly to you.

_____

_____

_____

Put your pen down. Sit quietly and listen for any new thoughts or what you sense the Lord is asking of you.

Respond with a written prayer of praise and thanksgiving.

_____

_____

_____

_____

YOUR READING

✤

Psalm 18:2

"The Lord is my rock, and my fortress, and my deliverer; my God, my strength, in whom I will trust; my buckler, and the horn of my salvation, and my high tower."

✤

Before you begin, take a moment to prepare your heart and mind.

Get in a quiet space. Clear your mind. Pray and invite God into this time.

Slowly read the Bible passage several times. Take your time.

Read quietly. Read out loud. Write it down.

_____

_____

_____

Note the words or phrases that speak to you.

Do not analyze. Just notice them.

Reflect on the word or phrases. What do they bring to mind?

Ask God to clarify and speak clearly to you.

_____

_____

_____

Put your pen down. Sit quietly and listen for any new thoughts or what you sense the Lord is asking of you.

Respond with a written prayer of praise and thanksgiving.

_____

_____

_____

_____

Prayer Request

Date: _____

_____
_____
_____
_____

Answered Prayer

Date: _____

_____
_____
_____
_____

Reflections

Date: _____

_____
_____
_____
_____

YOUR READING

✤

Psalm 27:1

"The Lord is my light and my salvation; whom shall I fear? the Lord is the strength of my life; of whom shall I be afraid?"

✤

Before you begin, take a moment to prepare your heart and mind.

Get in a quiet space. Clear your mind. Pray and invite God into this time.

Slowly read the Bible passage several times. Take your time.

Read quietly. Read out loud. Write it down.

_____

_____

_____

Note the words or phrases that speak to you.

Do not analyze. Just notice them.

Reflect on the word or phrases. What do they bring to mind?

Ask God to clarify and speak clearly to you.

_____

_____

_____

Put your pen down. Sit quietly and listen for any new thoughts or what you sense the Lord is asking of you.

Respond with a written prayer of praise and thanksgiving.

_____

_____

_____

_____

YOUR READING

❖

Nahum 1:7

"The Lord is good, a strong hold in the day of trouble;

and he knoweth them that trust in him."

❖

Before you begin, take a moment to prepare your heart and mind.

Get in a quiet space. Clear your mind. Pray and invite God into this time.

Slowly read the Bible passage several times. Take your time.

Read quietly. Read out loud. Write it down.

_____
_____
_____

Note the words or phrases that speak to you.

Do not analyze. Just notice them.

Reflect on the word or phrases. What do they bring to mind?

Ask God to clarify and speak clearly to you.

_____
_____
_____

Put your pen down. Sit quietly and listen for any new thoughts or what you sense the Lord is asking of you.

Respond with a written prayer of praise and thanksgiving.

_____
_____
_____
_____

Prayer Request

Date: _____

_____
_____
_____
_____

Answered Prayer

Date: _____

_____
_____
_____
_____

Reflections

Date: _____

_____
_____
_____
_____

YOUR READING

✣

Psalm 23:1—3

"The Lord is my shepherd; I shall not want. He maketh me to lie down in green pastures: he leadeth me beside the still waters. He restoreth my soul: he leadeth me in the paths of righteousness for his name's sake."

✣

Before you begin, take a moment to prepare your heart and mind.

Get in a quiet space. Clear your mind. Pray and invite God into this time.

Slowly read the Bible passage several times. Take your time.

Read quietly. Read out loud. Write it down.

_____
_____
_____

Note the words or phrases that speak to you.

Do not analyze. Just notice them.

Reflect on the word or phrases. What do they bring to mind?

Ask God to clarify and speak clearly to you.

_____
_____
_____

Put your pen down. Sit quietly and listen for any new thoughts or what you sense the Lord is asking of you.

Respond with a written prayer of praise and thanksgiving.

_____
_____
_____
_____

Ways God has blessed me

_____
_____
_____
_____
_____
_____
_____
_____
_____
_____
_____
_____
_____
_____
_____
_____
_____
_____
_____
_____
_____

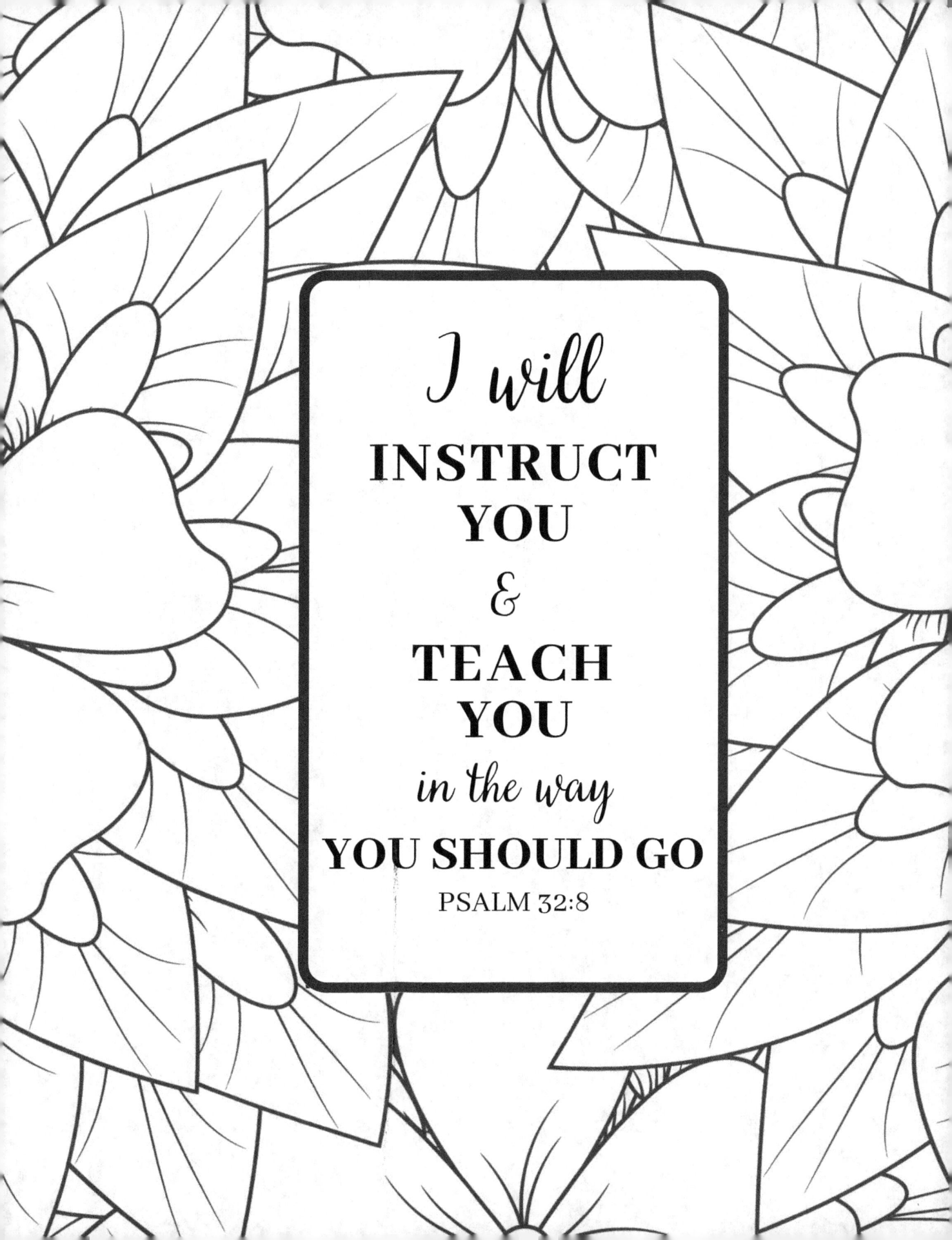

YOUR READING

2 Timothy 1:7

"For God hath not given us the spirit of fear; but of power, and of love, and of a sound mind."

Before you begin, take a moment to prepare your heart and mind.

Get in a quiet space. Clear your mind. Pray and invite God into this time.

Slowly read the Bible passage several times. Take your time.

Read quietly. Read out loud. Write it down.

_____
_____
_____

Note the words or phrases that speak to you.

Do not analyze. Just notice them.

Reflect on the word or phrases. What do they bring to mind?

Ask God to clarify and speak clearly to you.

_____
_____
_____

Put your pen down. Sit quietly and listen for any new thoughts or what you sense the Lord is asking of you.

Respond with a written prayer of praise and thanksgiving.

_____
_____
_____
_____

Lord, help me to

People I'm praying for today

YOUR READING

✠

Isaiah 12:2

"Behold, God is my salvation; I will trust, and not be afraid: for the Lord JEHOVAH is my strength and my song; he also is become my salvation."

✠

Before you begin, take a moment to prepare your heart and mind.

Get in a quiet space. Clear your mind. Pray and invite God into this time.

Slowly read the Bible passage several times. Take your time.

Read quietly. Read out loud. Write it down.

_____
_____
_____

Note the words or phrases that speak to you.

Do not analyze. Just notice them.

Reflect on the word or phrases. What do they bring to mind?

Ask God to clarify and speak clearly to you.

_____
_____
_____

Put your pen down. Sit quietly and listen for any new thoughts or what you sense the Lord is asking of you.

Respond with a written prayer of praise and thanksgiving.

_____
_____
_____
_____

Times I stepped out on faith

List the times you were afraid, but trusted God and you succeeded

YOUR READING

✜

Jeremiah 29:13

"And ye shall seek me, and find me, when ye shall search for me with all your heart."

✜

Before you begin, take a moment to prepare your heart and mind.
Get in a quiet space. Clear your mind. Pray and invite God into this time.

Slowly read the Bible passage several times. Take your time.
Read quietly. Read out loud. Write it down.

_____
_____
_____

Note the words or phrases that speak to you.
Do not analyze. Just notice them.

Reflect on the word or phrases. What do they bring to mind?
Ask God to clarify and speak clearly to you.

_____
_____
_____

Put your pen down. Sit quietly and listen for any new thoughts or what you sense the Lord is asking of you.

Respond with a written prayer of praise and thanksgiving.

_____
_____
_____
_____

Ways God has blessed me

_____
_____
_____
_____
_____
_____
_____
_____
_____
_____
_____
_____
_____
_____
_____
_____
_____
_____

YOUR READING

✣

Isaiah 41:10

"Fear thou not; for I am with thee: be not dismayed; for I am thy God: I will strengthen thee; yea, I will help thee; yea, I will uphold thee with the right hand of my righteousness."

✣

Before you begin, take a moment to prepare your heart and mind.

Get in a quiet space. Clear your mind. Pray and invite God into this time.

Slowly read the Bible passage several times. Take your time.

Read quietly. Read out loud. Write it down.

_____
_____
_____

Note the words or phrases that speak to you.

Do not analyze. Just notice them.

Reflect on the word or phrases. What do they bring to mind?

Ask God to clarify and speak clearly to you.

_____
_____
_____

Put your pen down. Sit quietly and listen for any new thoughts or what you sense the Lord is asking of you.

Respond with a written prayer of praise and thanksgiving.

_____
_____
_____
_____

YOUR READING

✣

Psalm 84:11

"For the Lord God is a sun and shield: the Lord will give grace and glory: no good thing will he withhold from them that walk uprightly."

✣

Before you begin, take a moment to prepare your heart and mind.

Get in a quiet space. Clear your mind. Pray and invite God into this time.

Slowly read the Bible passage several times. Take your time.

Read quietly. Read out loud. Write it down.

_____
_____
_____

Note the words or phrases that speak to you.

Do not analyze. Just notice them.

Reflect on the word or phrases. What do they bring to mind?

Ask God to clarify and speak clearly to you.

_____
_____
_____

Put your pen down. Sit quietly and listen for any new thoughts or what you sense the Lord is asking of you.

Respond with a written prayer of praise and thanksgiving.

_____
_____
_____
_____

Times I stepped out on faith

List the times you were afraid, but trusted God and you succeeded

YOUR READING

✣

John 14:18

"I will not leave you comfortless: I will come to you."

✣

Before you begin, take a moment to prepare your heart and mind.
Get in a quiet space. Clear your mind. Pray and invite God into this time.

Slowly read the Bible passage several times. Take your time.
Read quietly. Read out loud. Write it down.

_____

_____

_____

Note the words or phrases that speak to you.
Do not analyze. Just notice them.

Reflect on the word or phrases. What do they bring to mind?
Ask God to clarify and speak clearly to you.

_____

_____

_____

Put your pen down. Sit quietly and listen for any new thoughts or what you sense the Lord is asking of you.

Respond with a written prayer of praise and thanksgiving.

_____

_____

_____

_____

YOUR READING

✠

John 3:16

"For God so loved the world, that he gave his only begotten Son, that whosoever believeth in him should not perish, but have everlasting life."

✠

Before you begin, take a moment to prepare your heart and mind.

Get in a quiet space. Clear your mind. Pray and invite God into this time.

Slowly read the Bible passage several times. Take your time.

Read quietly. Read out loud. Write it down.

_____

_____

_____

Note the words or phrases that speak to you.

Do not analyze. Just notice them.

Reflect on the word or phrases. What do they bring to mind?

Ask God to clarify and speak clearly to you.

_____

_____

_____

Put your pen down. Sit quietly and listen for any new thoughts or what you sense the Lord is asking of you.

Respond with a written prayer of praise and thanksgiving.

_____

_____

_____

_____

Times I stepped out on faith

List the times you were afraid, but trusted God and you succeeded

_____
_____
_____
_____
_____
_____
_____
_____
_____
_____
_____
_____
_____
_____
_____
_____
_____

YOUR READING

✟

Psalm 27:1

"The Lord is my light and my salvation; whom shall I fear? the Lord is the strength of my life; of whom shall I be afraid?"

✟

Before you begin, take a moment to prepare your heart and mind.

Get in a quiet space. Clear your mind. Pray and invite God into this time.

Slowly read the Bible passage several times. Take your time.

Read quietly. Read out loud. Write it down.

_____

_____

_____

Note the words or phrases that speak to you.

Do not analyze. Just notice them.

Reflect on the word or phrases. What do they bring to mind?

Ask God to clarify and speak clearly to you.

_____

_____

_____

Put your pen down. Sit quietly and listen for any new thoughts or what you sense the Lord is asking of you.

Respond with a written prayer of praise and thanksgiving.

_____

_____

_____

_____

Lord, help me to

People I'm praying for today

YOUR READING

⁜

Hebrews 11:1

"Now faith is the substance of things hoped for,
the evidence of things not seen."

⁜

Before you begin, take a moment to prepare your heart and mind.

Get in a quiet space. Clear your mind. Pray and invite God into this time.

Slowly read the Bible passage several times. Take your time.

Read quietly. Read out loud. Write it down.

_____
_____
_____

Note the words or phrases that speak to you.

Do not analyze. Just notice them.

Reflect on the word or phrases. What do they bring to mind?

Ask God to clarify and speak clearly to you.

_____
_____
_____

Put your pen down. Sit quietly and listen for any new thoughts or what you sense the Lord is asking of you.

Respond with a written prayer of praise and thanksgiving.

_____
_____
_____
_____

Ways God has blessed me

_____
_____
_____
_____
_____
_____
_____
_____
_____
_____
_____
_____
_____
_____
_____
_____
_____

YOUR READING

✢

Psalm 139:14

"I will praise thee; for I am fearfully and wonderfully made: marvellous are thy works; and that my soul knoweth right well."

✢

Before you begin, take a moment to prepare your heart and mind.
Get in a quiet space. Clear your mind. Pray and invite God into this time.

Slowly read the Bible passage several times. Take your time.
Read quietly. Read out loud. Write it down.

_____
_____
_____

Note the words or phrases that speak to you.
Do not analyze. Just notice them.

Reflect on the word or phrases. What do they bring to mind?
Ask God to clarify and speak clearly to you.

_____
_____
_____

Put your pen down. Sit quietly and listen for any new thoughts or what you sense the Lord is asking of you.

Respond with a written prayer of praise and thanksgiving.

_____
_____
_____
_____

Prayer Request

Date: _____

_____
_____
_____
_____

Answered Prayer

Date: _____

_____
_____
_____
_____

Reflections

Date: _____

_____
_____
_____
_____

YOUR READING

✜

Matthew 7:12

"Therefore all things whatsoever ye would that men should do to you, do ye even so to them: for this is the law and the prophets."

✜

Before you begin, take a moment to prepare your heart and mind.
Get in a quiet space. Clear your mind. Pray and invite God into this time.

Slowly read the Bible passage several times. Take your time.
Read quietly. Read out loud. Write it down.

_____
_____
_____"_____

Note the words or phrases that speak to you.
Do not analyze. Just notice them.

Reflect on the word or phrases. What do they bring to mind?
Ask God to clarify and speak clearly to you.

_____
_____
_____

Put your pen down. Sit quietly and listen for any new thoughts or what you sense the Lord is asking of you.

Respond with a written prayer of praise and thanksgiving.

_____
_____
_____
_____

Ways God has blessed me

_____
_____
_____
_____
_____
_____
_____
_____
_____
_____
_____
_____
_____
_____
_____
_____

YOUR READING

✧

Isaiah 40:31

"But they that wait upon the Lord shall renew their strength; they shall mount up with wings as eagles; they shall run, and not be weary; and they shall walk, and not faint."

✧

Before you begin, take a moment to prepare your heart and mind.

Get in a quiet space. Clear your mind. Pray and invite God into this time.

Slowly read the Bible passage several times. Take your time.

Read quietly. Read out loud. Write it down.

_____
_____
_____

Note the words or phrases that speak to you.

Do not analyze. Just notice them.

Reflect on the word or phrases. What do they bring to mind?

Ask God to clarify and speak clearly to you.

_____
_____
_____

Put your pen down. Sit quietly and listen for any new thoughts or what you sense the Lord is asking of you.

Respond with a written prayer of praise and thanksgiving.

_____
_____
_____
_____

YOUR READING

───── ✤ ─────

Psalm 19:14

"Let the words of my mouth, and the meditation of my heart,
be acceptable in thy sight, O LORD, my strength, and my redeemer."

───── ✤ ─────

Before you begin, take a moment to prepare your heart and mind.

Get in a quiet space. Clear your mind. Pray and invite God into this time.

Slowly read the Bible passage several times. Take your time.

Read quietly. Read out loud. Write it down.

_____
_____
_____

Note the words or phrases that speak to you.

Do not analyze. Just notice them.

Reflect on the word or phrases. What do they bring to mind?

Ask God to clarify and speak clearly to you.

_____
_____
_____

Put your pen down. Sit quietly and listen for any new thoughts or what you sense the Lord is asking of you.

Respond with a written prayer of praise and thanksgiving.

_____
_____
_____
_____

YOUR READING

James 1:17
"Every good gift and every perfect gift is from above, and cometh down from the Father of lights, with whom is no variableness, neither shadow of turning."

Before you begin, take a moment to prepare your heart and mind.

Get in a quiet space. Clear your mind. Pray and invite God into this time.

Slowly read the Bible passage several times. Take your time.

Read quietly. Read out loud. Write it down.

_____
_____
_____

Note the words or phrases that speak to you.

Do not analyze. Just notice them.

Reflect on the word or phrases. What do they bring to mind?

Ask God to clarify and speak clearly to you.

_____
_____
_____

Put your pen down. Sit quietly and listen for any new thoughts or what you sense the Lord is asking of you.

Respond with a written prayer of praise and thanksgiving.

_____
_____
_____
_____

My Favorite Scriptures

My Favorite Scriptures

www.ingramcontent.com/pod-product-compliance
Lightning Source LLC
Chambersburg PA
CBHW060424010526
44118CB00017B/2354